ICE CREAM U

ICE CREAM U

The Story of the Nation's Most Successful Collegiate Creamery

Lee Stout

The Pennsylvania State University Libraries

University Park, Pennsylvania

This book was made possible in part through the generosity
of Ronald W. and Eleanor Judy Smith. Proceeds from the sale
of this book will be used to support the Penn State University
Libraries.

Frontis piece: Farm wagons, and one Model T, line up to
deliver milk and cream to the Creamery in Patterson Hall,
ca. 1910.

Library of Congress Cataloging-in-Publication Data

Stout, Lee.
Ice Cream U : the story of the nation's most successful
collegiate creamery / written by Lee Stout.
          p.   cm.
Summary: "Traces the history of the Creamery at The Pennsylvania State University, and examines issues relating to ice
cream production, the dairy industry, and agricultural education programs"—Provided by publisher.

Includes bibliographical references.

ISBN 978-0-615-24780-9 (cloth : alk. paper)
1. Creameries—Pennsylvania—History. 2. Dairy products
industry—Pennsylvania—History. 3. Ice cream, ices, etc.—
Pennsylvania—History. I. Title. II. Title: Story of the nation's
most successful collegiate creamery.

SF266.S76 2009
637.09748'53—dc22
2008043335

Printed in China by Everbest Printing Co.
through Four Colour Imports, Louisville, KY
Published by The Pennsylvania State University Libraries,
University Park, PA 16802

It is the policy of The Pennsylvania State University Libraries
to use acid-free paper. Publications on uncoated stock satisfy
the minimum requirements of American National Standard
for Information Sciences—Permanence of Paper for Printed
Library Material, ANSI Z39.48-1992.

This book is dedicated to all the students, staff, and faculty

who have worked for more than a century to make the Creamery

such a special place in the hearts of Penn Staters everywhere.

Acknowledgments

The writing of a history of the Creamery would not have happened without the wonderful generosity of Eleanor J. Smith and her late husband, Ronald W. Smith, who donated the funds to the University Libraries to enable this volume to be created and published. Mrs. Smith is the granddaughter of Creamery Superintendent Frank Knoll, who played a significant role in the development of the Creamery from 1905 to 1944. He supervised production, taught students, and worked with faculty to facilitate research and short-course work for the industry that built Penn State's unparalleled reputation for excellence in dairy science and ice cream production in particular.

I would like to thank Nancy Eaton, dean of University Libraries and Scholarly Communications; Michael Furlough, assistant dean for scholarly communications; William L. Joyce, Huck Chair and head of special collections; and Shirley Davis, assistant to the dean for external relations, for conceiving of the project and asking me to be a part of it. Catherine Grigor, University Libraries public information and marketing director, and Patrick Alexander, University Press associate director and editor-in-chief, played key roles in developing the project. At University Publications, Karen Magnuson, assistant director; Sally Heffentreyer, editor; Erin J. Wease, designer; and Fred Weber, photographer, were invaluable to making this volume as attractive and readable as it is. Jackie Esposito, University archivist, and assistants Paul Dyzak, Robyn Dyke, and Alston Turchetta were extraordinarily helpful in locating necessary primary source materials for the book. Travis Edwards of the Penn State Dairy Barns and Professor Emeritus Daryl K. Heasley, curator of the Pasto Agricultural Museum, were both very helpful in enabling us to take and identify photos for the book.

Especially vital to the creation of this history has been Creamery Manager Thomas Palchak, whose enthusiasm and cooperation continue to energize me. Food Science professors emeriti Philip Keeney and Manfred Kroger were both extremely generous with their time and assistance. All three of these marvelous gentlemen read the manuscript at various stages and provided important new information and corrections for my misunderstandings and omissions. Finally, my wife, Dee, read every draft of this work and offered endless encouragement and suggestions for its improvement. It would not have been possible without her help and patience.

— *Lee Stout*

Contents

Above: Weather vane from College Dairy Barn, now preserved at the Pasto Agricultural Museum, Rock Springs

Left: Penn State Dairy Barns, constructed in 1915, on the site of today's Agricultural Administration Building

Inset: State College Dairy milk wagon, ca. 1900

Introduction

It's a crisp Homecoming afternoon, with an amber sun glinting off pumpkins and fallen leaves. The Nittany Lions have won (of course) and no after-game glow seems right without an ice cream cone from the Creamery. As you wait in line with the other alums, you mull over the flavors. No question, you have to do it. It just can't be anything but Peachy Paterno.

This could be the quintessential Penn State moment, but it could also be …

A winter morning and you're staggering to that 8 o'clock class in the Forum from your East Halls dorm. No time for breakfast? Hold on, it's twenty to eight and there's the Creamery. Should you go for a bagel with cream cheese? A carton of milk? Oh, wait—a WPSU Coffee Break milkshake sounds like the way to get the motor running. Can a sugar buzz last for a whole class period? Twenty-five degrees out … OK, the shake will stay cold on the way to class.

Or could it be …

Early May—the last days of classes. The rain has finally stopped. The sun has been shining for two or three days in a row and the temperature climbs to almost seventy. It's what you've been waiting for. Every tree seems to be exploding with new leaves. Get out and walk, and while you're at it, what could possibly be better than ice cream? With all the flowering trees bursting into bloom, Cherry Quist seems like the perfect choice.

Or perhaps …

A warm, muggy July evening on Old Main lawn. Arts Festival has drained your stamina and now you're content to look up at the stars and listen to the music. Hmm, the people on the blanket next to you have just brought back dishes of ice cream. Gosh, that looks good, and so you wander over to the Creamery tent by the Obelisk. What to choose … the chocoholic fever rises. Only one answer—Keeney Beany Chocolate.

If any of these scenes resonate with you, then you have tasted the magic of the Penn State Creamery and its incredible ice cream. How is it that a humble ice cream cone vies for icon status with JoePa and the Nittany Lion Shrine? What is so unique about Penn State's Berkey Creamery, now housed in the new Food Science Building that causes it to grow when other college creameries have been shrinking or disappearing altogether? What draws business professionals from all over the world to Penn State to learn the secrets of ice cream making in our famous Ice Cream Short Course? How did we become "Ice Cream U," as more than one journalist has called us?

Penn State is famous for many accomplishments, beautiful campuses, outstanding faculty and students, successful alumni, and much more. This book concentrates on one of its most popular achievements—the Creamery—and how it has become one of Penn State's great success stories. We hope you enjoy this taste of Penn State.

The four Hall of Fame flavors: (left to right) Cherry Quist, Peachy Paterno, WPSU Coffee Break, and Keeney Beany Chocolate

❶ Penn State's Role in the Growth of Pennsylvania's Dairy Business

Why does Penn State have a creamery? The simple answer is that milk and other dairy products are Pennsylvania's number-one agricultural commodity and, thus, the research, teaching, and outreach mission in support of dairy has always been a primary focus of Penn State's College of Agricultural Sciences. Despite the fact that many people view Pennsylvania as an industrial state, farming is still vital to the economy, with agricultural production valued at more than $4.2 billion. Dairy represents one-third of that output and Pennsylvania is ranked number four in

Creamery milk cans at Pasto Agricultural Museum

the country in dairy production. The history of Pennsylvania agriculture and Penn State's contributions to it provides a useful backdrop for the story of the development of the Penn State Creamery.

Europeans' appetite for dairy products goes back thousands of years. Their discovery of the New World didn't change that, but it presented a problem. Native Americans had no domesticated herding animals, so the Europeans brought their cows, oxen, goats, and sheep with them to these new settlements. In Pennsylvania, the first colonists were the Swedes in 1638, followed by the Dutch, and then William Penn and his fellow English Quakers in 1682. They introduced an ever-greater diversity of population to Pennsylvania, with Welsh, Scots-Irish, and especially German immigrants finding tolerance in the province for their various religious beliefs.

This variety of cultures naturally brought an array of farming practices as well. But thanks to the settlers' skills and the marvelous fertility of the Piedmont soils of southeastern Pennsylvania, the colony soon became a highly productive farming area. These farmers not only fed their own families, but were also able to export surplus grain and flour, making Pennsylvania the "breadbasket" of the American colonies.

The Germans, in general, were the most productive farmers and the most skilled in raising livestock. They were more accustomed to a harsher climate than the English and Scots-Irish and built "Schweizer" bank barns...which protected their cattle and allowed for winter feeding...

Holstein cows, the farmers' favorite breed today

The expansion of the railroads in southeastern Pennsylvania, beginning around 1830, gradually provided a means for Philadelphia and other urban centers to acquire more fresh fruits and vegetables from surrounding counties. This also meant a growing market for dairy products.

Over these years, settlement gradually expanded to northern and western Pennsylvania. There, farmers found lower-quality soils and shorter growing seasons. This area lacked the rich fertile ground of the southeastern Piedmont and the limestone valleys of central Pennsylvania and few crops could prosper there. Raising cattle for both beef and milk soon became the predominant type of farming in these areas. By midcentury, competition from Ohio and states farther west pushed Pennsylvania out of the grain export business. From the 1850s on, Pennsylvania farmers increasingly turned their attention to livestock, and especially the dairy cow.

The Germans were generally the most productive farmers and the most skilled in raising livestock. They were more accustomed to a harsher climate than the English and Scots-Irish and built "Schweizer" bank barns (based on barns used in the upper Rhine Valley and in northern Switzerland), which protected their cattle and allowed for winter feeding, while other groups simply left their cows out during the winter to fend for themselves. Butter and cheese were the primary products, since fluid milk spoiled before it could get far from the farm.

In the first half of the nineteenth century, farm production gradually became more balanced between farm crops and livestock. Early farmers had tended to deplete their land and then move west to new areas; by 1800, there were abandoned farms and thousands of idle acres in the southeast. Gentlemen farmers, particularly the members of the Philadelphia Society for Promoting Agriculture, a scientific society that included George Washington and Benjamin Franklin as members, promoted soil improvement through crop rotation and fertilizing with lime and manure. This yielded better feeds, and combined with better breeds of cattle and improved care of the animals, livestock production increased. By the 1840s both beef cattle and dairy products, mainly butter and cheese, were growing in importance.

Traditionally, handling the dairy was a woman's role on the farm. In fact, the word "dairy" comes from the Middle English word *deyerie*. The *dey* was the farm woman, and the *-erie* suffix referred to the place that was her domain, thus it was where the farm wife did her work. And work she and her children did! They fed, cared for, and milked the cows, carried the milk to the spring house, put it in crocks or tin pans set in cold water, skimmed the cream off when it had risen, churned the cream, worked the resulting butter, rinsed off the buttermilk to feed to the pigs, salted and packed the butter, and took it off to market to sell.

Coed with Ayrshire cow at the college barns, ca. 1915. The white and red Ayrshires were first brought from Scotland to New England in the 1830s because they were hardy in the cool climate and good producers.

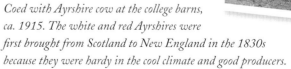

After the Civil War (1861–1865), dairy operations began to modernize—with mechanical refrigeration after 1875, mechanical cream separators starting in 1879, and surge milking machines after 1920. Thus began the industrialization of the creamery, as commercial butter factories were then called. By 1880, factory butter was outpacing farm-made butter in sales. Cheese factories, which had begun in upstate New York in the 1850s, also came to Pennsylvania in the 1860s. Often they were added to butter factories, and production alternated between the two, which increased efficiency.

This was just the beginning of modern dairy farming and production in Pennsylvania. Greater quantities of market milk began to be shipped into cities from adjacent communities in the 1870s, but it was an unsavory business at first. Neither the wholesalers who bought the farm milk and sold it to consumers nor the farmers knew or cared much about sanitation or purity. Milk was frequently bacteria-contaminated from both farm and milk plant, and was often watered down by the milkman. Nevertheless, better transportation, refrigeration, sanitation, pasteurization, cattle inspections to combat disease, and even the introduction of the milk bottle in 1878, all improved the product. By 1900 market milk replaced butter and cheese as the most important and profitable product for the dairy farmer.

Another dairy product also saw its introduction in this period. Ice cream has a considerable history (which will be addressed later), but it began to appear in cities and towns in larger quantities in the 1850s. It quickly became popular and its growth was phenomenal after 1900. Around 1930, it was reported that Pennsylvanians consumed 50 million gallons of ice cream annually, or about five gallons per person. Pennsylvania produced 14 percent of the nation's ice cream, and Philadelphia was judged the ice cream capital of the nation.

These hand-cranked centrifugal cream separators are part of the collections of Penn State's Pasto Agricultural Museum. They became common on dairy farms and in creameries beginning in the 1880s, rapidly increasing the production of cream and the consistency of the product.

Pennsylvania agriculture was changing irrevocably. In 1840, the Commonwealth had 128,000 farms operating on 14 million acres. By 1900, thanks to the appetite of Pennsylvania's growing population, this had increased to 224,000 farms on 19 million acres. With the coming of the twentieth century, however, Pennsylvania farm numbers started to decline in competition with industrial growth and urban living. Today, only 58,000 farms operate on about 7.6 million acres. Farm population has also declined from about a million people living and working on farms around 1900 to perhaps 700,000 in 1950 to fewer than 300,000 today.

Yet Pennsylvania farm production has never been stronger, and dairy products are the leading component. Of $4.3 billion in sales of Pennsylvania farm products in 2002, dairy represented $1.4 billion, twice as much as any other type of farm product. In fact, Pennsylvania ranks only behind California, Wisconsin, and New York in dairy production. Let's now turn to the role that Penn State has played in the evolution of Pennsylvania's agricultural and dairy industry.

Penn State began as the Farmers' High School of Pennsylvania. The act of 1855 that incorporated the farm school was the result of lobbying by the Pennsylvania State Agricultural Society. Founded in 1851, many of the new organization's leaders also were active members of the Philadelphia Society for Promoting Agriculture, which had been encouraging education and experimentation since its founding in 1785.

The founding vision of the Farmers' High School was to apply science to improve agriculture, a task the society believed existing colleges could not do. They were too costly and the "character of education" they provided was inappropriate. The new agricultural school's students would learn those aspects of science practical for a farmer to know.

The college's first quarter-century was unsettled, to say the least. After a location in Centre County was chosen for the campus, an economic depression brought a halt to construction of the college building. After more than a year of inaction, a curriculum was planned, faculty hired, students admitted, and classes begun in February 1859. By the fall, the new president, Dr. Evan Pugh, arrived to take charge. The institution's first 100 students were on their way.

Pugh was one of a few Americans at that time with a science Ph.D. earned in Germany. In addition, he had studied European agricultural education models, and was working in the world's first agricultural experiment station in England. Pugh's research had earned him international recognition in the scientific community.

Penn State had begun its interest in dairy work as early as 1865, with its first cows and a small dairy structure.

He was, for his time, a world-class researcher, and the perfect man to oversee the new school.

Pugh also removed any confusion over the school's status by changing its name in 1862 to the Agricultural College of Pennsylvania, which helped secure its designation as the state's recipient of funding from the Land Grant

Above:
Students plowing with mules in front of unfinished Old Main, ca. 1860

Right: Unfinished Old Main as the first students might have seen it in the winter of 1859

College Act of 1862 (also known as the Morrill Act). Unfortunately, Evan Pugh died unexpectedly in 1864 at the age of 36 and, without his strength and vision, the college languished for the next seventeen years.

It was not until George W. Atherton took the helm in 1882 that Penn State began to develop into a strong and successful collegiate institution. Atherton

First creamery structure, Ag Hill, had room for butter- and cheese-making instruction and little else

tion would hamper the agriculture student, taking him out of the realm of solid, practical farming. It was not until the turn of the century that Dr. Henry Prentiss Armsby, dean of Penn State's School of Agriculture and director of the Experiment Station, crafted an educational program that realized the vision of the founders. His objective was not scientific farmers, but rather agricultural scientists, whose research findings could then be communicated to the state's farmers.

An 1889 state appropriation included $7,000 for the college's first academic creamery building.

Armsby himself would play a key role in popularizing Penn State with the Commonwealth's farmers through his own particular specialty—the study of animal nutrition and the feeding of livestock for maximum productivity. His research became known throughout the country, if not the world, and his *Manual of Cattle-Feeding* (1902), became mandatory reading for the state's dairy farmers.

Penn State had begun its interest in dairy work as early as 1865, with its first cows and a small dairy structure. Later, two small herds of dairy cows were kept to study feeds and production and to provide milk for simple creamery work. The ag school's experimental work largely focused on fertilizer analysis, but also included feeding experiments with animals. Bulletins reporting research results began to be issued under President Atherton in 1882. There was considerable interest in this work, and even in 1885, the bulletin mailing list had 10,000 names. In 1887, the Agricultural Experiment Station was created and dairy work began to concentrate on Ag Hill, as the northeast area of campus came to be called.

An 1889 state appropriation included $7,000 for the college's first academic creamery building. This simple, one-story structure, located near today's Ferguson Building, contained a cold-storage room, cream-ripening room, and general workroom. It hosted both instruction and research in dairy manufacture by William J. Caldwell, the first Penn State instructor in the field. A small herd of Guernsey cows, which produced high-fat milk that was good for butter and cheese, was also added at this time.

increased enrollments and hired more faculty, thanks primarily to developing interest in engineering programs. Penn State began to receive regular legislative appropriations. Even with these positive steps, agriculture had not resurfaced the way Pugh had intended.

While Pugh may have understood the importance of applying science to agriculture, it was not clear to others. In fact, many believed that "too scientific" an educa-

The earliest research examined the effect of temperature on the rising of cream when the milk was set. Traditionally, it was thought that cooling the milk by setting the tins in cold water enhanced the cream production, but it was learned that the important variable was actually the breed of cow from which the milk came. At the same time, investigators also learned that manure and other foul odors in the barn could infiltrate the sitting cream and reduce the quality of the resulting butter.

This small building also made possible, in 1892, the initiation of two dairying short courses: an eight-week course for creamery-men held in January and February, and a four-week course in March for private dairy owners. These courses were rigorous, emphasizing butter making, milk testing and milk chemistry, along with cow feeding and management. Ice cream making was also part of the January course, and thus instruction in ice cream making traces its roots at Penn State to 1892, making it the first collegiate institution to offer instruction in the field. Correspondence instruction also began here in the same year, and would later include a variety of dairy courses.

One of the first advances was testing for milk-fat content using the Babcock test. Developed at the University of Wisconsin, this first scientifically reliable test replaced determining milk fat by eye and taste with a scientifically derived percentage of fat. This enabled dairies to price products more uniformly and develop standards in production.

The experiment station published the first major creamery-related bulletin in 1892, titled "Tests of Dairy Apparatus." This involved work with several different mechanical cream separators, which began to be developed in 1879. Continuously

Dairy short course students separating cream (right) and churning butter (left), 1894

centrifuging the milk to separate the cream was not only faster, but also produced cream with a considerably higher milk-fat content and thus better-quality butter.

The Creamery soon was producing more dairy products than were needed on campus. As far back as 1869, records show that the college farm sold small quantities of milk at eight cents a quart, probably to neighboring farmers for butter making. By the 1890s, milk from the dairy herd was being made into butter on campus, but community demand was such that additional cream was also purchased from nearby farmers, yielding an output of 1,600 pounds a week. Our college butter was even exhibited with other Pennsylvania dairy products at the 1893 World's Columbian Exhibition in Chicago, receiving high marks.

Dairy experimental work focused on both fundamental and practical research. Faculty, staff, and students would investigate the science of dairy production and its products as well as their manufacture, to provide information for both the farmer and the commercial producer. Penn State's agricultural scientists began serious study of the chemistry of milk and its constituent components, the fermentation of milk for cultured products, the physiology of milk secretion, the basics of both butter and cheese formation, the composition and structure of milk and butter fats, and methods of milk analysis and of testing of fluid milk products to determine the milk-fat content. Another important part of the work of the experiment station continued to be testing foods for adulteration. Agricultural chemist William Frear was often called to testify for the state's Dairy and Food Commission about the purity of manufactured foods. To his dismay, he sometimes found evidence that water was added or lethal chemicals such as boric acid or formaldehyde to serve as preservatives in some milk sold in the state.

Another aspect of this concern for purity came with the controversy over oleomargarine. This inexpensive spread made of oils, animal fats, and skimmed milk was usually made colorless but the unscrupulous sometimes added yellow food coloring and sold it as butter. The legal battles began in the 1870s, but attempts to control labeling, to tax it, or to ban it outright all failed. By the turn of the century, the dairymen's frustration led to the creation of the state Dairy and Food

Commission. Ultimately, margarine could not be kept off the market as a cheap substitute for butter and it is still sold as such today, outselling butter about threefold.

With all the work being done for instruction, research, and the short courses, the 1889 Creamery was drastically overcrowded. The small rooms housed a variety of pieces of equipment for use and evaluation as well as the regular separation of cream, butter, and occasional cheese making. An addition to the Creamery containing an ice house did not solve the space problems, and the work overflowed to the basement of the adjacent experiment station building, where milk testing was carried out.

The flow of thousands of copies of bulletins, well-attended events during Farmers' Week, fundamental research in both nutrition and feeding of dairy cows, scientific analysis of milk and dairy products, and evaluation of new methods of testing and manufacturing made Penn State's "dairy school" increasingly valuable to the Pennsylvania dairymen and manufacturers. In just four years, enrollments in the short course for creamerymen rose to thirty-seven and in the course for dairy owners to fourteen. The success of the program and the value of its work were becoming self-evident. As farm organizations pressed the state for new agriculture facilities at the college, there seemed little question that an expanded dairy building was crucial enough to be the first priority.

The state recognized the importance of dairy farming with the construction of the Patterson Building in 1904. The installation of modern equipment to study and improve dairy manufacturing became a key part of that work, and ice cream would play a central role in Penn State's contributions to this new and growing industry.

"Safe Milk" pamphlets produced by Penn State Dairy Husbandry Department to persuade consumers that milk, "the perfect food," improves nutrition, ca. 1920

② A Brief History of Ice Cream

Take some snow or crushed ice, mix in flavoring, honey, or fruit, and you probably have the original frozen dessert. It's likely that the Greek and Roman elites, and perhaps Chinese emperors and Indian sultans could enjoy such a treat centuries ago. But at some point, likely in the seventeenth century, someone introduced cream into the mix and we were on our way to modern ice cream.

Of course, you can't have ice cream without freezing and so the history of ice cream is closely associated with the development of refrigeration techniques, including the use of ice houses or ice wells to keep ice through the warm months. Probably also in the seventeenth century, people discovered that mixing salt into snow and ice enhanced the cooling of whatever they touched. The ice cream maker, invented in the mid-nineteenth century, marked the turning point in the history of ice cream, and mechanical refrigeration, developed by the end of the nineteenth century, made possible the development of the ice cream industry.

Certainly the American taste for ice cream owes much to Thomas Jefferson. A recipe for French vanilla ice cream in Jefferson's handwriting is part of his collected papers and can be seen on the Library of Congress' Web site.

While many legends are told about ice cream makers at European courts, such as England's Charles I providing a pension for his French chef to keep his favorite ice cream recipe a secret and Catherine de Médici's taking Italian chefs to France in the sixteenth century, where they created crèmes and sorbets, there is no evidence for these stories. But ice cream was enjoyed in France and England at least by 1700 and ice cream recipes were published in French and English cookbooks in 1768 and 1769, respectively.

An early mention of colonial ice cream appears in 1744 in the *Journal of William Black*. Virginia commissioners on their way to negotiate a treaty with the Iroquois stopped at the home of Maryland governor Thomas Bladen. Black, one of the commissioners, reported that their dining was concluded with "a Dessert no less Curious; … some fine Ice Cream which, with the Strawberries and Milk, eat most Deliciously."

Certainly the American taste for ice cream owes much to Thomas Jefferson. A recipe for French vanilla ice cream in Jefferson's handwriting is part of his collected papers and can be seen on the Library of Congress' Web site. He apparently acquired this recipe while he was the U.S. minister to France in the 1780s, and ice cream then became a favored treat at Monticello. The ingredients were: two bottles of good cream, five egg yolks, ½-pound of sugar, and a vanilla stick. The recipe calls for hand mixing and finishes with the ice cream being chilled in a mold surrounded by ice, a practice with a long history of its own.

Beginning in 1789, when New York City was briefly the national capital, First Lady Martha Washington served ice cream at her weekly receptions. Abigail Adams, the wife of the vice president, reported Martha Washington and the president greeted all the ladies and then, "The company are entertained with Ice creems & Lemonade." A merchant later noted that, according to his records, Washington spent about $200 for ice cream that summer.

Ice cream continued to be a favorite dessert for the wealthy and powerful, but with the broader availability of ice, it could become a more popular treat for the masses. Philadelphia, with its many ice cream parlors, became the best-known center for the frozen treat. Among those distributing in the city in 1832 was Augustus Jackson, an African American who had been a White House chef and is credited with first using ice mixed with salt to chill his mix. He distributed his numerous ice cream varieties in tin cans to the many ice cream shops in the city.

The modern era arrived with the invention of the hand-cranked ice cream freezer by Nancy M. Johnson, for which she received a U.S. patent in 1843. Her machine is essentially the same design used today in home ice cream freezers, but it was revolutionary because it enabled almost anyone to make high-quality ice cream at home, thanks to a new and inexpensive commodity called rock salt.

Not long after, the first ice cream wholesaler appeared in Baltimore in 1851. Jacob Fussell, a milk dealer, also made and sold ice cream at twenty-five cents a quart using milk from York County farms. He later expanded his operations to Washington and Boston. This was still a niche market, though, with only 4,000 gallons of ice cream made nationally in 1850.

The Centennial Exhibition of 1876 in Philadelphia drew tourists from all over and spread the fame of Philadelphia ice cream. Bakers who created edible cups for ice cream also contributed to the popularity of the city's ice cream. However, the 1904 World's Fair in St. Louis deserves credit for popularizing the rolled waffle cone filled with ice cream. By 1909, an automatic cone-rolling machine was invented, and cone production skyrocketed thereafter.

Ice cream was well on its way by the turn of the twentieth century, with 5 million gallons produced in 1899, 30 million by 1909, and 150 million by 1919. Mechanical refrigeration was well established with the invention of the brine freezer in 1902. In 1925, the first commercially successful continuous-process ice cream freezer was invented and mass production truly took off.

By World War II, ice cream was considered vital to the war effort. Americans cut back on it at home because of rationed ingredients, but it was available to the troops overseas. When the aircraft carrier *Lexington* was sinking during the Battle of the Coral Sea in 1942, its sailors gathered all the cans of ice cream they could find and ate them before abandoning the ship. By the end of the war in 1945, the Navy commissioned a barge for ice cream making to be used in the Western Pacific that could produce ten gallons of ice cream every seven seconds.

Ice cream has a fascinating history, and Penn State plays a significant role in that history through its creamery, research, and educational programs.

Traditional hand-cranked ice cream freezer

③ Patterson Hall and the Community Dairy Business

In 1900, Pennsylvania's agricultural associations met in State College at the call of Agriculture Dean Henry Prentiss Armsby. His premise was that the college required their help. The need for new buildings, equipment, and faculty was urgent. They agreed and formed a loose coalition called the Allied Agricultural Organizations. It would work with the Pennsylvania Department of Agriculture to lobby for higher appropriations for Penn State, as well as advocate for a high school in every township, a rural road network, and nature education classes in public schools.

One of the first outcomes of these efforts came in 1903, when the legislature appropriated $100,000 for a new dairy building. Completed in 1904, it was a substantially larger structure than the old Creamery. (It was named for longtime farm superintendent William Calvin Patterson in 1926.) Its two stories included classrooms, offices, laboratory space, and an expanded Creamery space for what became, in 1907, a separate Department of Dairy Husbandry (later renamed Dairy Science). Three years later, the department developed options in dairy production and dairy manufacturing to match growing specialization in the industry.

Department head Herbert Van Norman diversified the college's herd of Guernseys with purebred Jerseys, Holsteins, and Ayrshires, and also established the annual Farmers' Week, which showed off the school and provided new information to farmers in 1907. At the same time, the department hired one of the few women faculty members in the school. Elizabeth B. Meek, a Bellefonte native who had done graduate work at the University of Chicago, joined the faculty in 1907 and taught bacteriology to both undergraduates and short-course students.

The new building provided considerably more space for milk testing and dairy bacteriology, which had begun to receive more prominence. Cows in the college herd had been routinely tested for bovine tuberculosis since the test was developed in 1892, and in 1895 a State Livestock Sanitation Board was created to enforce testing across the state, where as many as 25 percent of the herds were thought to be infected. The danger of tuberculosis from the milk or meat of contaminated animals was a major public health risk, and Penn State worked very hard to help diminish it.

A State College Creamery delivery wagon being loaded at the Patterson Building, the new Dairy Husbandry and creamery building, in 1905

Dairy farmers line up their wagons to sell their cream and milk to the State College Creamery.

The creamery facility in Patterson included a small sales space, rooms and new equipment to produce bottled milk, butter, cheese, and ice cream, as well as laboratories for both milk testing and bacteriology. The research work continued to aid both farmers and manufacturers. These included studies of milking machines, moisture and other factors in butter making, and bacteria in milk. Butter research was considered especially important because Pennsylvania led the nation in butter production in the early 1900s.

As noted earlier, the Creamery had begun to sell its dairy products and in 1902, had created a milk route in the surrounding community to deliver fluid milk, butter, and cheese. With the growing demand, the Creamery began to buy more cream and milk from nearby dairy farmers. By 1908, the State College Creamery, as it was then called, was obtaining cream and milk from 100 different farms in the county. The Creamery's butter was sold in Philadelphia and Scranton, while cream was wholesaled in Bellefonte and Tyrone. Just four years later, total receipts

By 1908, the State College Creamery, as it was then called, was obtaining cream and milk from 100 different farms in the county.

were $69,700 and 195 farmers were supplying the Creamery with cream and milk.

Penn State enrollments were booming in the years preceding World War I, having risen from approximately 600 in Atherton's last year (1906), to more than 2,500. The legislature, however, was not keeping up with the college's space needs, although it did provide a stock judging pavilion and a new Swiss-style dairy barn by 1915. All dairy cows were now brought together in the new barns on the location of what today is the Agricultural Administration Building.

A familiar Ag Hill scene of those days was the horse-drawn wagons and motorized trucks of local farmers delivering ten-gallon cans of cream and milk to the Patterson Building creamery. Sales in 1914 were nearly $85,000, and milk and cream came from 256 farms. The demand led to the purchase of new equipment for pasteurizing and cooling. Penn State milk bottles, first introduced in 1904, were also an important part of what we would today call the "branding" of the Creamery. Initially labeled "State College Dairy," both the bottles and the horse-drawn delivery

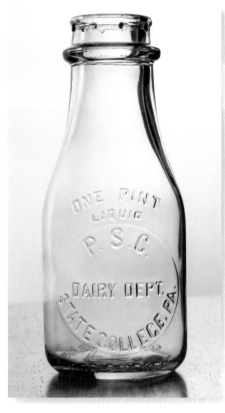

Glass bottles improved sanitation for fluid milk and were introduced at the Creamery in 1904. The bottle on the preceding page dates from that time, while bottles on this page show an evolving style of identification from about 1918 to the mid-1940s. These bottles are now on display at the Pasto Agricultural Museum and are part of the collection donated by Dr. Darwin Braund '56, past curator of the museum.

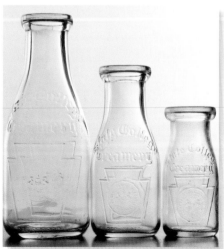

wagon were identified with a "State College Creamery" logo by 1914. A year later, the Creamery produced 150,000 pounds of butter and almost 5,500 gallons of ice cream. One of the early Experiment Station bulletins to deal with ice cream appeared then, examining methods to influence the body and texture of ice cream.

With the end of World War I, Penn State's Dairy Husbandry department had a new head, Andrew Borland, who came in 1919 and served until 1948. The college creamery was still growing and by 1925, production had reached 228,000 pounds of butter, 25,000 pounds of cheese, 36,000 gallons of ice cream, 250,000 quarts of milk, and 32,500 quarts of cream.

The 1920s saw an increase of ice cream-related research, especially with the hiring of two new faculty members in dairy manufacturing, Chester D. Dahle in 1924 and F. J. Doan in 1926. Together they were responsible for the majority of the research done on ice cream and other dairy products. Among the topics they examined were effects of the percentage of butterfat and solids in ice cream, aging of the ice cream mix, the introduction of powdered stabilizers, studies of variations in homogenization and pasteurization, the effects of acidity of the ice cream mix, and the first studies of cocoa and chocolate milk and ice cream.

By the start of the 1930s and the onset of the Great Depression, new studies in milk marketing and agricultural economics became more prominent with the worldwide declines in agricultural prices, demand, and productivity. Yet the growing numbers of faculty, students, research projects, and creamery production had long outstripped the facilities of the Patterson Building. In 1931, construction began on a new dairy building and creamery, which would open in 1932 and later be known as Borland Laboratory. Its location just across the road, but closer to the dairy barns, was a more efficient site, and the increase in space was urgently needed. Patterson continued to be used for dairy bacteriology work and became the home of the Agricultural Library.

It was in Borland Lab that the fundamental character of the Creamery changed from a commercial dairy operation to the campus-centered facility we know today.

Top: Farmers unload milk at Patterson, 1920s. Bottom: Drivers and fleet of Creamery delivery trucks at the Borland Lab loading dock, 1950s.

④ Ice Cream Short Course

Dairy short-course students outside the first creamery building with their instructor in cream separation and buttermaking, H. B. Gurler, 1893

How does an agricultural college convey the results of its scientific research to farmers? Ever since land-grant colleges first experimented with various fertilizers to see which would give the best crop yields,

"There will be no charge for tuition, but an incidental fee of $3.00 will be levied, and books will cost about $3.00."

By the late nineteenth century, news of experiments in farm magazines had evolved into the experiment station research bulletin. But there was also a need to provide concentrated instruction and hands-on practice to farmers. They could not take years off to be regular students, but they could afford a few weeks in the winter, when farming chores were greatly reduced. Thus, the short course was born.

Although earlier, general courses failed to attract a broad enough audience, the college, in 1891, decided to try a course for dairy farmers emphasizing milk production and a course for creamerymen emphasizing manufacturing. These courses succeeded and courses were soon added in other areas, including cheese making.

getting out the good news has been a challenge. Perhaps the earliest means was the farm magazine, which began to gain popularity among gentlemen farmers in the 1830s. As county and statewide agricultural organizations developed soon thereafter, publications such as the *Pennsylvania Farm Journal* (for which Evan Pugh wrote) were being read by more than just wealthy gentlemen farmers.

From the farm associations came the fairs, exhibitions, and demonstrations that historically have played a role in outreach. Anyone who has attended Penn State's Ag Progress Days or the Pennsylvania State Farm Show knows that this continues to be true today.

Students in 1901 were told: "Each student in the Creamery course will be required to provide himself with two white suits and caps, to be worn at all exercises in the creamery and milk-testing laboratory, and one set of blue jeans for shop work.

"All participants in the course will attend twenty lectures on Butter, Ice-Cream and Dried Curd Manufacture, five lectures on Dairy Chemistry and Milk-Testing, eight lectures on Dairy Feeding, eight lectures on Dairy Cattle, their Care and Management,

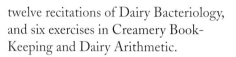

Left: Short-course students pose with their instructors at the Beaver Field grandstand, ca. 1906 (H. P. Armsby, top row, third from left).

Below: Mr. Gurler teaches Creamerymen's short course students to rate butter in taste test, 1894.

twelve recitations of Dairy Bacteriology, and six exercises in Creamery Book-Keeping and Dairy Arithmetic.

"There will be no charge for tuition, but an incidental fee of $3.00 will be levied, and books will cost about $3.00."

In 1992, a special conference was held to mark the centennial of the ice cream short course. One of the speakers, Wilbur A. Tharp, a student in the 1923 Dairy short course, recalled his experiences with the eight-week curriculum. He noted that by then, lectures on dairy cattle and dairy feeding were long gone and the course included the following variety of subjects:

— Milk: receiving, bottling, storage, and distribution

— Milk marketing

— Bacteriology

— Cheese manufacture: cottage, Cheddar, Limburger, etc.

— Ice cream: mix formulation and manufacture, freezing and flavoring, and storage and tasting

— Butter making and buttermilk

— Dairy refrigeration and bookkeeping

Students were working eight hours a day, six days a week in class, the laboratory, and the manufacturing facilities of the Creamery, and had homework to do in the evening as well. The dairy manufacturing course became so popular that a condensed version of the ice cream portions of the course began to be offered separately starting in 1925.

One year earlier, in 1924, Dr. Chester D. Dahle, professor of Dairy Manufacture, took over the short course. With the Great Depression, few farmers or production men could afford an eight-week course and enrollments fell. During World War II, most short-courses were reduced to two weeks, popularly called "shotgun" courses around the college. After the war, the creamery course was split into three successive courses: Testing Dairy Products and the Manufacture of Butter and Cheese, Ice Cream Making, and Market Milk and Milk Control.

In addition to the specialized two-week ice cream course, there was also a one-week course for salesmen, who provided ingredients to the many local Pennsylvania dairies and ice cream plants. By the postwar period, more than 3,000 students had taken courses and worked in dairy plants throughout the nation. In 1949, ages of students ranged from 16 to 60 and more than 200 men and women applied for only 60 spaces. The students came from every state in the union, and three international students were also in attendance from British Columbia, Canada; Nicaragua; and Shanghai, China. What accounted for its success? Dahle believed that it was the hard work of the instructors and the quality of the equipment and management of the Creamery. He concluded, "There's no other college in the country, and probably the world, which puts on a short course to rival the one here."

"There's no other college in the country, and probably the world, which puts on a short course to rival the one here."

Dahle retired suddenly in 1955, but fortunately someone was ready to step in and take over, Dr. Philip G. Keeney. He would follow Dahle's thirty-one years with a thirty-year tenure of his own in running the ice cream short

Top: The first short-course instruction in pasteurization, 1894. It was hoped then that this new process would halt the spread of diseases through milk and cream.
Bottom: Students preparing to make cheese, ca. 1920

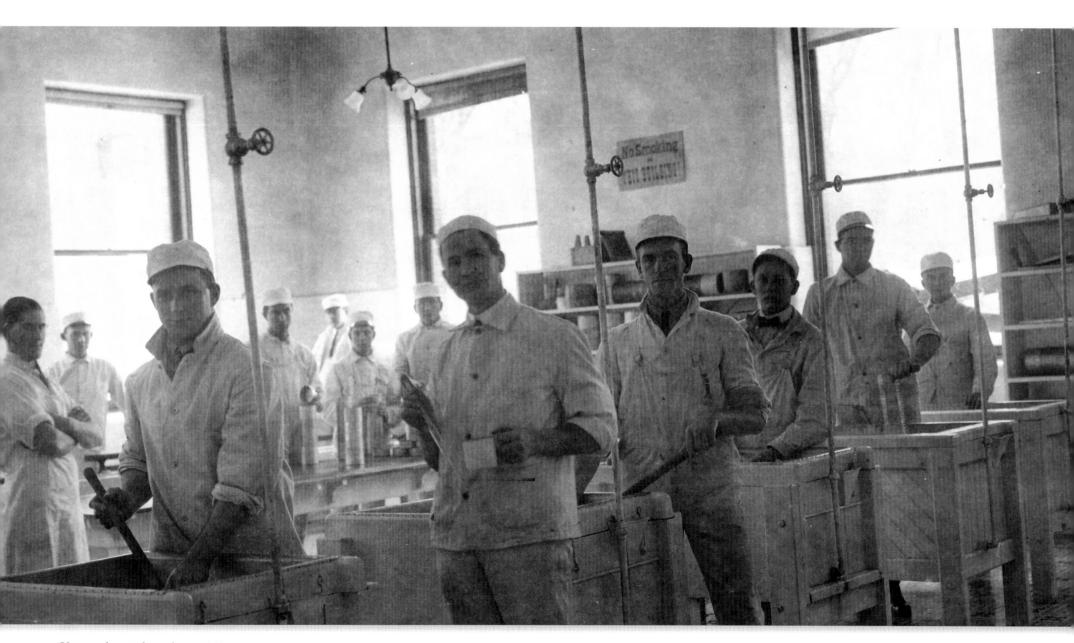

Cheese makers at the ready, ca. 1920

Students in Borland's labs determining milk fat from fluid milk samples, ca. 1935

course (1955–1985). Keeney continued the traditional strengths of the course, but also updated it regularly, adding new aspects such as large-plant manufacturing, marketing, ice cream novelties and other new products, entrepreneurship in retail manufacturing, and use of computers in all phases of manufacturing and testing.

Keeney saw dramatic changes in the ice cream market during his years. When he started in 1955, most ice cream businesses were small family-owned, all-purpose dairies that sold to local groceries, shops, and drug stores. But big changes were coming. The rise of large supermarkets and grocery chains, and the improvement of home refrigerators and freezers meant the demand for ice cream rose. Small dairies consolidated and fewer people were interested in the short course. By the 1970s, however, new players were advancing in the market. So-called "dip stores" like Baskin-Robbins were opening shops everywhere, as drug store soda fountains disappeared. Gourmet ice creams like Häagen-Dazs, the faux-Danish treat made in the Bronx with 16 percent milk fat, were becoming popular. Ben & Jerry's, "home-made by two Vermont hippies," brought a counter-culture sensibility to super-premium ice cream. Cows grazed on the front lawn of their Waterbury, Vermont, facility, where visitors were welcome to tour the plant and get free ice cream.

With the new cachet that ice cream was earning, industry's support of the course strengthened and numbers of attendees expanded from the 50 to 60 range in the 1950s to more than 100 and sometimes 150 by the 1990s. Representatives of virtually every major ice cream maker sent people to Penn State, including Baskin-Robbins, Borden, Breyers, Häagen-Dazs, Hershey's Ice Cream, and Good Humor. While Ben Cohen eventually came for the course, too, Ben & Jerry's began in 1977 with the correspondence version of the short course for a $5 fee—their class papers are on display for tourists to see in their plant!

Penn State was not alone in offering short courses in dairy work and even ice cream, but most of the colleges that offered them have either dropped them or de-emphasized them since the 1930s as numbers of dairy farmers and manufacturers declined. Some colleges felt that these hands-on courses were less attractive than focusing on more basic science and seeking federal grants. Today, only a handful of schools offer a course like Penn State's, but none with the history or depth of this one.

In 1985, Dr. Arun Kilara took over supervision of the course and continued until his retirement in 1997, when Dr. Robert Roberts took over. Keeney and Kilara con-

Dairy short-course students milk the college herd, ca. 1920.

tinue to teach in the short course. Today's students certainly receive a more modern approach to ice cream manufacture than their 1923 counterparts. The course now includes: characteristics of ice cream and frozen desserts consisting of ingredients and processes, flavors, freezing and hardening, and storage and distribution; manu-facturing systems, including microbiology and quality control, sanitation, regula-tions, and hazard analysis; and laboratory demonstrations of ice cream freezing, computer-assisted formulation, and sensory evaluation—aka tasting!

Attendance continues to hold steady, ranging from 110 to 130, with sometimes as many as 150 students. The course now has more than 4,000 graduates and its international reputation has continued to grow, with students attending from every continent except Antarctica. Versions of the course with Penn State instructors par-ticipating have been conducted in places as far away as Australia, with Kilara over-seeing it. At the 1992 Centennial Conference, the sentiment was expressed that "the Penn State Ice Cream Short Course is nothing less than the best in the world" and there seem to be few if any who would argue the point. Besides Creamery patrons, it makes you wonder just how many cones of ice cream around the world can trace their roots back to the Ice Cream Short Course!

⑤ Borland Lab and Ice Cream Sales

In June 1932, the Department of Dairy Husbandry moved into the newly constructed $500,000 Dairy Building, which would eventually bear the name of the department head, Andrew Borland (after his death in 1958). The new three-story building was designed in a "T" shape, facing west. The top of the "T" contained offices and classrooms, while the rear wing, the bottom of the "T," housed the Creamery. Its milk delivery entrance faced the dairy barn, directly east across Shortlidge Road. According to Dairy Manufacturing Professor Chester D. Dahle, it was "the finest college creamery in America from the standpoint of arrangement, convenience, and facilities for instructional purposes."

It provided ample room for students to work and observe in both regular classes and short courses. The Creamery had separate rooms for making butter, cheese, market milk, ice cream, and condensed milk and milk powder. The butter room housed a 1,000-pound-capacity device to churn, salt, and work butter into one-pound "prints." Top-grade milk went through filtering, pasteurizing, cooling, and bottling before it was delivered to customers.

Milk not needed for bottling was separated into cream and skim milk or used for cheese. Some cream was bottled for consumers, but most was used for ice cream. Skim milk was used for cottage cheese or condensed milk and cultured buttermilk. Most of the cheese made in the Creamery was cheddar, although they also made some "Philadelphia style" cream cheese, pimento and relish cheese in dishes, and, of course, cottage cheese.

The ice cream, containing 14 percent milk fat, was pasteurized, homogenized, flavored, and cooled before being transformed in the freezer. Ice cream was made in three different types of freezers then, only one of which was a continuous freezer as is used today. The Creamery also had three ammonia compressors to provide refrigeration and the freezing capacity to harden and store the ice cream.

Borland Lab was designed with as many modern features as possible, including all service lines entering the building from tunnels that ran throughout the campus. Unfortunately, heavy rain in 1933 opened large cracks in the building's north end. Two sinkholes were found below the basement floor, each four feet wide and fifteen feet deep, along with a thirty-five-foot crevice running under three main columns supporting the north end of the building. This "unsettling" discovery cost a further $100,000 to repair as a new foundation and heavy-duty bracing were added to provide the building with more support.

The Creamery, under the strong management of Frank Knoll since 1905, employed twelve full-time workers and any number of students part-time who also helped to produce dairy products for the market place. Demand was strong and the Creamery still bought milk from some 300 farms in the region, although the change to storing milk in refrigerated bulk tanks on the farm, a process pioneered by Penn State researchers in the 1950s, would dramatically reduce the number of small dairy farmers. Throughout the 1940s and '50s, delivery routes, covered by a small fleet of Penn State Creamery trucks, ranged as far as Altoona.

A young Frank Knoll in 1905, soon after relocating to State College, where he managed the Creamery

Dr. Andrew Borland lays the cornerstone for the building that would eventually bear his name, 1931. On that same day, he placed a time capsule in the wall, which was opened in 2006. The contents—documents, photographs, and publications from 1931—were placed in the University Archives.

It could not last, however. As early as 1937, private dairies had protested to their state legislators that the Creamery represented unfair competition. Penn State was running a commercial dairy, and even though it was an auxiliary enterprise (a self-supporting operation using no state funding), it still paid no taxes. The 1959 decision to halt home deliveries had some origins in Harrisburg, but was also recognition that with the growing dormitory presence on campus, more than 10,000 student spaces built in the 1950s and early '60s, the Creamery had a major job to supply milk and other dairy products to just the growing student body. At that time, it filled more five-gallon milk cans for dining hall dispensers than any dairy in the country.

From then on, the Creamery restricted itself to what it could sell on campus—to the dining halls, The Nittany Lion Inn, the HUB, and in the Creamery's own small, second-floor salesroom in 110 Borland Lab. However, with the end of home deliveries, the Creamery needed a larger and more visible sales room to build its walk-in business. This was accomplished with the construction of the familiar glass-walled sales room along Curtin Road, on the south side of Borland's Creamery wing in 1961. From figures available, the Creamery made about 44,000 gallons

Butter Making

Creamery Practice

Top: Students making butter in Patterson Building, ca. 1920

Bottom: "Creamery practice" includes chilling cream for butter-making in Patterson Building, ca. 1920.

Dairy and Creamery Building
Pennsylvania State College

Above: The completed Borland Laboratory on a picture postcard

Left: The lobby of Borland Laboratory in its early days, 1935

of ice cream in 1957–58 and it would appear that by 1962–63, with the new salesroom well established, ice cream production had increased by almost 50 percent.

Even in that 1957–58 period, the Creamery made twenty-four flavors of ice cream, with vanilla, chocolate, and bittersweet mint being the top three sellers, representing about 55 percent of all production (nationally, vanilla, chocolate, and strawberry were the top three at about 73 percent of the market). By 1968, the Creamery made approximately 65,000 gallons and by the early 1980s, ice cream production had risen to almost 90,000 gallons a year.

Instruction and research in Borland Lab had continued to grow and prosper throughout the 1930s, '40s, and '50s. Queries from industrial associations and dairy and food companies were frequently the basis for investigations. These covered a wide variety of areas of dairy manufacturing, including protein stability and vitamin fortification; the development of new products, such as low-carbohydrate ice cream for diabetics; practical storage issues, including freezing, dehydration, and shrinkage of the ice cream in the carton; and with Stuart Patton, who became the department's most distinguished researcher, studies in food flavors and flavoring.

Early students making cheese, ca. 1900

Typical butter-making equipment used on dairy farms, ca. 1915

Student making ice cream in Patterson, ca. 1920

Analytical testing by faculty in Patterson, 1937

Students testing milk fat in Borland Lab, 1937

Dairy students judging cows in the Stock Judging Pavilion, now the Pavilion Theatre

Above and right: Bacteriology lab in Patterson, ca. 1936

The Agriculture Library in Patterson Building

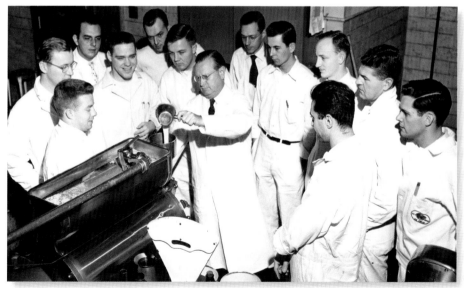

Professor Dahle and ice cream-making students, 1940s

Much of the ice cream research continued under Chester Dahle, who also headed the Ice Cream Short Course, and Francis J. Doan. They were joined in the 1940s by Donald Josephson, who would eventually head the Department of Dairy Husbandry for twenty-seven years, overseeing its transition to Dairy Science in 1954, the formation of the Department of Food Science in 1975, and the merger of Dairy and Animal Science in 1976. In 1955, Dahle retired and was replaced by Philip G. Keeney, a newly minted Ph.D., who took over his instructional load in both regular courses and the short course.

With the 1944 retirement of Frank P. Knoll, who served the Creamery as superintendent for almost forty years, five successors over the next forty-two years, Ray Yoder, George Dreibelbis, Bill Coleman, John Foley, and Ray Binkley, brought the Creamery steadily along. A close working relationship existed with Dairy Science, and in particular the faculty who taught the dairy courses, Dahle, Doan, George Watrous, Edward Glass, and especially Keeney, for most of those years. While the Creamery may have seemed like an independent enterprise during those years, it never deviated from its primary function in support of instruction and research, and as a service to industry and the public.

Ron Ross, sales supervisor, in the original Borland "dairy store," second floor, ca. 1952

Students in the 1940s line up for sodas at the fountain in the original Borland sales room.

PROPOSED
DAIRY SALESROOM
BORLAND LABORATORY

DRAWN BY	DEPARTMENT OF	SCALE
J.M.C.	PHYSICAL PLANT PLANNING AND CONSTRUCTION	
DATE 5-8-59	THE PENNSYLVANIA STATE UNIVERSITY UNIVERSITY PARK, PA.	SHEET 1 OF 5

The new Creamery Sales Room in architect's perspective and as finished and in use, 1960

Above: Umbrellas, tables, and chairs in the patio areas outside the new sales room add to customer comfort.

Left, top: Visiting ministers take time out from their Town & Country Pastor's conference for a not-so-sinful treat, 1948.

Left, bottom: Ice Cream short-course students work at the freezers, bringing forth new batches of ice cream.

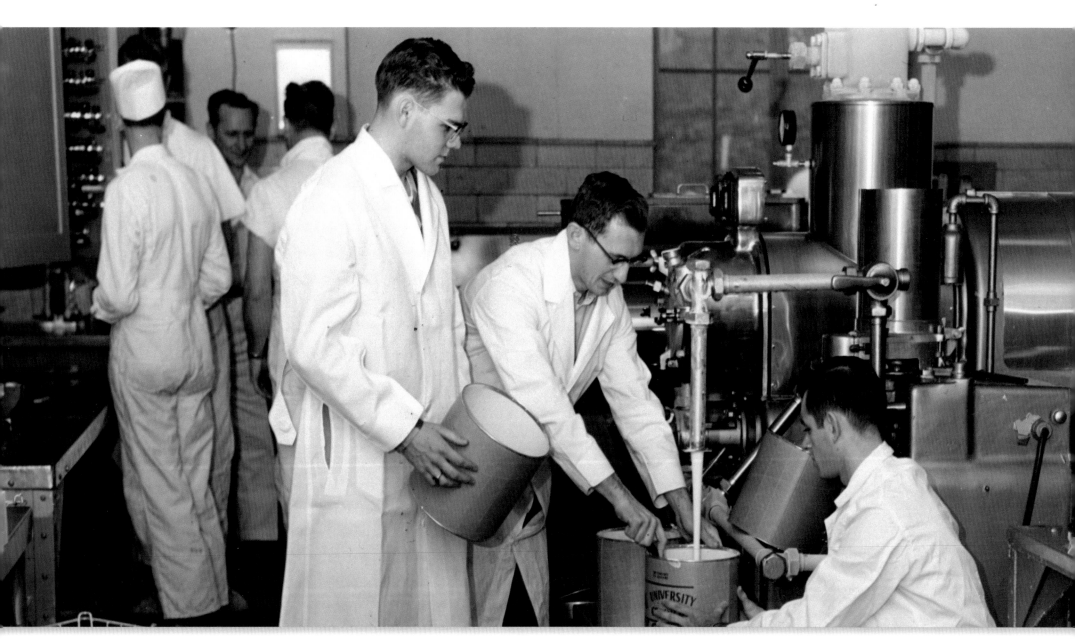

Creamery ice cream pours from the freezer in Borland Lab's ice cream production room, ca. 1960

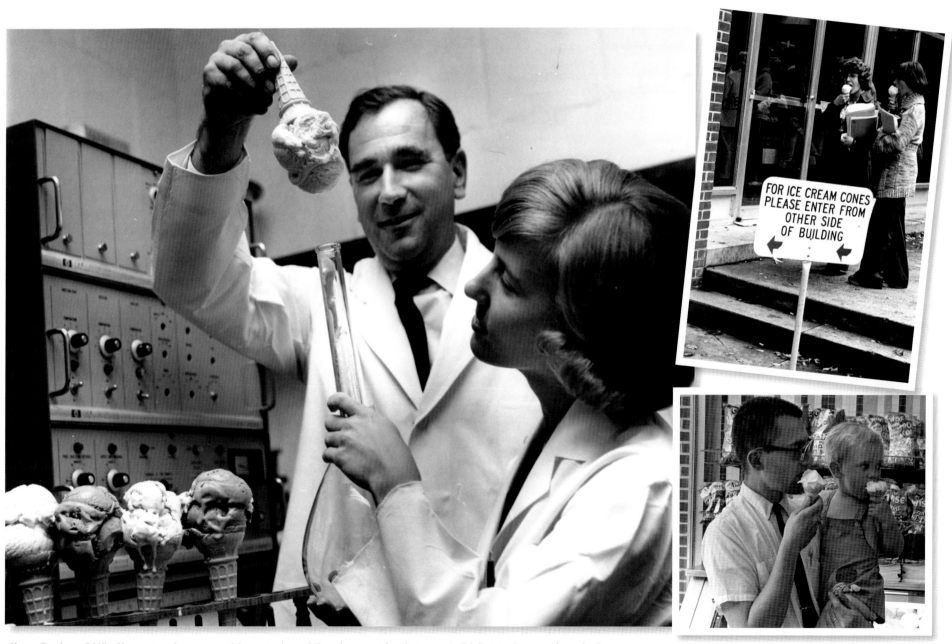

Above: Professor Philip Keeney tests ice cream melting capacity, while assistant catches drops, 1967. Right top: As a cone from the Creamery became more popular, queuing instructions became necessary, ca. 1978. Right bottom: No dad can resist giving his little one an ice cream cone.

Home delivery had been financially tenuous and after it ceased the Creamery began to accumulate surplus income, which it used to buy new equipment and support some of the lab work for students.

With the creation of the Department of Food Science in 1975, the dairy faculty most closely associated with the Creamery moved from Dairy Science into the new Food Science program. However, the Creamery became more closely integrated with the Food Science Department in 1987, with the hiring of the new Creamery manager, Thomas Palchak.

Palchak led the operation through a dramatic turn-around ... the revitalized Creamery energized the faithful, following a path of continuous innovation and strong marketing.

Tom Palchak, Creamery manager since 1987

By that time, Palchak discovered the Creamery was in desperate need of new equipment, as requirements for expensive new research equipment and construction of new dairy barns had drawn off surpluses. In fact, some existing equipment appeared to be barely functional, and there had also been some declines in quality and in production. Penn State followed national trends for a time with a decline in milk consumption in the dining halls on campus.

In some ways, this mirrored the state of the industry—small dairies had been going under since the 1950s and plants were becoming ever-larger operations run by fewer companies. Between 1970 and 2005, the number of plants making regular hard ice cream in the nation decreased from 1,628 to 354, while actual production grew from 762 million gallons to 960 million gallons. Similar decreases were also seen in numbers of plants for fluid milk and cheese making. As a result, the numbers of jobs and students were declining as well. This contributed to a change in many land-grant colleges from production-oriented dairy departments to broader and more research-oriented food science departments.

At Penn State, even the dining halls were buying less from the Creamery, and the number of flavors of ice cream being made and sold was less than fifteen. Food Science faculty cautioned the College of Agriculture that without new equipment and a major investment in the facility, the Creamery might have to close. However, Palchak led the operation through a dramatic turnaround. He renewed staffing to rebuild quality, production, and revenues. He persuaded the College of Agriculture and the University to loan the Creamery $3 million for renovations and replacement of old, worn-out major equipment.

The seven-year loan was repaid in three, as the revitalized Creamery energized the faithful, following a path of continuous innovation and strong marketing. Computers were added to monitor and control the operation of the continuous-process machinery. The flavor list began to expand again, including the first cookies-and-cream flavor, an instant hit created by students in a food product development class. A host of other flavors followed and today there are more than 150 varieties in the Creamery's repertoire, with about twenty-five to thirty available at any time. The Creamery also expanded its product line, adding new low-fat flavors, as well as bottling its own iced tea and orange juice.

At Penn State, the Creamery warrants a historical marker. Originally placed at Borland, the marker was recently updated and moved to the new building.

Growth was remarkable: From a $1.75 million budget in 1987, the Creamery budget now approaches $5 million. A significant part of this success has been the remarkable public profile the Creamery has developed. In the late 1980s, a syndicated children's television show, *Capelli and Company*, came to the Creamery and filmed a feature on ice cream making. Then came *Mr. Rogers*, which was followed by a glowing newspaper story by the *Pittsburgh Post-Gazette*'s food editor and a visit by popular columnist Erma Bombeck, doing a feature for ABC-TV's *Good Morning America*.

The hall-of-fame flavor Peachy Paterno, introduced in 1987, became a regular topic on Penn State football television broadcasts. The subject really took off when former Pittsburgh Steeler Lynn Swann did an entire feature for a football broadcast from the Creamery plant, where they just happened to be making a special "Swann Swirl" ice cream flavor for the network crew. The ball kept rolling with Martha Stewart, the Food Network, and Rick Sebak's *An Ice Cream Show* for public

television. The national press covered President Bill Clinton sitting down in 1996 at the Creamery for a one-time only, two-flavor, two-scoop ice cream cone. What marketing genius could have dreamed that up? Incredibly, no marketing genius and no marketing plan are in place at the Creamery. It buys no advertising. "Word of mouth" has a very special meaning when it comes to Creamery ice cream.

President Bill Clinton joins President Graham Spanier for a cone at the Creamery. President Clinton is the only person to ever receive a two-flavor cone from the Creamery.

37

⑥ The Ice Cream Phenomenon

In a survey conducted by the Penn State Alumni Association in the early 1990s, the University Creamery was the second-most-recognized institution at the University, after football. That is an incredible finding and yet nobody is all that surprised. Anyone who has spent any amount of time at Penn State will have encountered Creamery ice cream as a follow-up to innumerable activities. Any Penn State Alumni Club, regardless of location, will tell you its events generate more excitement if there is the promise of scoops of Creamery ice cream at the meeting. But it's not a secret held near and dear only by Penn Staters of every stripe.

What is it that makes the humble ice cream cone both mythic and iconic for Penn State?

We have become "Ice Cream U" to the news media. *The New York Times, Pittsburgh Post-Gazette, Harrisburg Patriot, Philadelphia Inquirer*, and all manner of smaller newspapers, magazines, and trade journals over the years have found the Creamery to be newsworthy.

No footage shot for broadcast of a documentary about ice cream is complete without a stop at the Creamery to explain how ice cream is made. If the planning is done well enough in advance, a visit to January's Ice Cream Short Course is included, to show the teaching of ice cream making. Whether it's *Pennsylvania Factory Tours* for the Pennsylvania Cable Network or *Modern Marvels* on the History Channel, television has visited the Creamery on a regular basis.

How did this happen? What is it that makes the humble ice cream cone both mythic and iconic for Penn State? We've recounted something of the history of ice cream and a good deal about the evolution and development of Penn State's modern creamery operations. Perhaps we need to briefly consider how milk fits into this picture.

Very few kids can resist Creamery ice cream.

Obviously, not everyone drank milk in the past, nor does everyone drink it today. Some scholars believe that the majority of the world's population, the so-called "non-herding cultures," lose their enzymatic ability to digest milk comfortably after infancy. Is the ability to tolerate lactose in the digestive tract a mutation that only some of us have happily inherited? We may never know. Many societies have no tradition of adults drinking the milk of cows, goats, or any other animals. However, the northern European herding cultures, as author Margaret Visser puts it, "reserved a special awe for milk; it is a food more than a drink, and it is innocent, pure, white, and wholesome. To freeze cream with fruit and sugar is to add an extra dimension of delight to the solid worth of milk."

Left: Scooping cones and dishes still represents the primary activity for the expanded Berkey Creamery.

Half-gallon containers stored in the Creamery freezer are ready to go home.

Like milk, ice cream has a number of cultural characteristics that we associate with it. Pure, cold, clean, refreshing, and comforting, ice cream draws us in. There is a nostalgic feeling to eating ice cream; it takes us back to childhood, the country, green grass, and cows. It can conjure up a memory, real or imagined, of a family gathering around a hand-cranked freezer, and being the one who gets to lick the fresh ice cream off the dasher. Ice cream, in its simple cone, and its capacity to melt suggests a treat that can exist only in the here and now; it's a food that we have to stop everything else to eat. It suggests relaxation and crowds on vacation taking a cone in the afternoon.

If we've sensed these feelings in ice cream marketing, that's no accident. The dairy business has been suggesting to us for decades that milk is the perfect food: a natural, universally loved source of nutrition and good health. Of course, it wasn't always so, but that doesn't seem to spoil the feeling. In 2006, the United States consumed 1.5 billion gallons of frozen desserts, almost two-thirds of which was regular ice cream. We seem to enjoy the paradox that the American fitness craze and passion to be thin began in earnest in the 1970s, at the same time that the country was discovering super-premium ice cream with its 16 percent milk fat. Some describe ice cream as almost an addictive drug, but as one author put it, it's the "innocent drug"—an antidote to anxiety over the stress to be thin. If you go off your diet, what better way to do it than with ice cream? It has become a national guilty pleasure.

Setting aside the emotional connection, what keeps us stuck on ice cream is the taste. Ice cream has always seemed an exquisite taste fantasy. Europeans treated it as a luxury, an elegant dessert for the elite, with creamy and rich tastes that seemed to fit in easily with the tradition of fine confectionaries and candies. Stendhal, the nineteenth-century French writer, remarked after tasting ice cream for the first time, "What a pity this isn't a sin." Americans made ice cream democratic and available to everyone. Immigrants arriving at Ellis Island were given ice cream on their first day in their new country. It may well be a symbol of national identity for Americans.

For Penn Staters, ice cream has become symbolic as well. Most alumni can easily recall stopping by the Creamery for a cone … often. With the University's enrollment now around 42,000 at University Park alone, Penn State has become a very big place. Thus, the desire among Penn State students to connect has grown as well, and that strong sense of connectedness stays with them after they graduate. How else could we explain the world's largest college alumni association and how that ice cream cone on a campus visit renews so many golden memories?

Just as the Creamery as symbol has grown in importance, so also has its reputation as an educational enterprise, thanks in large part to the Ice Cream Short Course. The length of service of the four professors who have been in charge of the course since the 1920s—Dahle, Keeney, Kilara, and Roberts—has been extraordinary. The public attention that Keeney, in particular, garnered for the course has been amazing. Hailed by a national magazine as the "Emperor of Ice Cream" and given credit for raising the popularity of ice cream in China and several European countries, Keeney contributed greatly to Penn State's exceptional world ice cream profile.

Combine the depth of emotional attachment, a food product that tastes so good and that Penn State handles so well—on the teaching side, better than anyone else in the world, judging by the international recognition of the Ice Cream Short Course—and it is easy to understand why Penn Staters love the Creamery and that undisputed champion of dairy products, Creamery ice cream.

If there's ice cream to be eaten, send in the clowns! Ringling Brothers circus staff can't resist the lure of the Creamery.

⑦ The Berkey Creamery and the Future

Borland Lab was nearing its seventieth birthday in 2002 and one fact was becoming painfully obvious. The Creamery, and its parent Department of Food Science, were desperately out of space. There was no room for any new equipment and storage was at such a premium that most Creamery supplies were kept in other buildings. At the same time, the infrastructure was rapidly approaching crisis status. The electric supply to the building was overtaxed, and steam lines and the refrigeration plant were outmoded. The Creamery was ready for a new home. In fact, soon after the Creamery moved to its new quarters a steam line to Borland collapsed, closing Curtin Road for a number of weeks.

A new mall in the making—the Class of 2007's senior class gift was thirty-one American Tulip trees that will line the promenade that has the Arboretum as its focal point

In August 2006, the Berkey Creamery opened in the new $46 million Food Science Building, named for Earl K. and Jeanne Claycomb Berkey '47, lead donors for the project. At 3,700 square feet, the new sales and seating area is two-and-a-half times the size of the Borland Lab salesroom. Besides being more spacious, with seating for about 100, the new sales area is a modern space, yet it has touches of nostalgia, with an ice cream parlor feel, from the glass-topped cases where student workers scoop cones and dishes to the white-topped tables with wood and metal chairs. The new Creamery is close to Beaver Stadium, swimming pools, the Bryce Jordan Center, Eisenhower Auditorium, and a variety of other Penn State attractions. With its comfortable outdoor seating area, it's positioned at the foot of a "green" mall that flows north between the Business and Forest Resources Buildings, along a promenade shaded by tulip poplars donated by the Class of 2007, and leads to the new Arboretum.

Above: Patio seating at the new Berkey Creamery

Right: Dr. Spanier greeting the Berkeys as they arrive in their namesake facility for a preview in June 2006

Facing page: The Creamery and its production plant are front and center on the first floor of the new Food Science Building.

Above: Milk vats hold product before it enters the production stream.
Right: Gallon jugs swirl through the production line on the way to being filled with Creamery milk.

The 130,000-square-foot Food Science Building design, largely overseen by department head John Floros, was approved in 2004 and construction commenced soon after. The Creamery salesroom and production facility share the ground floor with the department's wet and dry pilot plants, which are used for instruction and research in the practical aspects of food equipment. The upper three floors include offices, classrooms, and laboratories, along with special spaces such as the Sensory Lab, and lab spaces for food chemistry, food processing, research instrumentation, food microbiology, and food sample preparation.

The heart of the facility can be seen through glass windows. The 25,000-square-foot Creamery processing plant, which houses $7.1 million in new equipment, generated in its first year of operation 250,000 gallons of milk, 36,000 pounds of sour cream, 50,000 pounds of ricotta cheese, 125,000 pounds of cream cheese, 60,000 pounds of cheddar cheese, 90,000 pounds of yogurt, and 225,000 gallons of

Milk quickly fills the gallon jugs, which are capped, labeled, and moved on to cold storage.

Cheese production area in the new Creamery Plant

ice cream. That's enough ice cream for three-quarters of a million cones and dishes, with a fair amount left over for bulk sale in the Creamery and shipment to the dining halls, HUB, Nittany Lion Inn, and Penn Stater restaurants, not to mention thousands of overnight mail orders for ice cream packed in dry ice sent throughout the continental United States.

At a national meeting of college creamery managers and staff held at Penn State during the summer of 2007, one of Tom Palchak's counterparts, after viewing the new facility and observing the strong sense of ownership and passion Penn Staters have for their Creamery, said, "I leave here thinking of all the things that you have and all the things that we don't have. I can't believe how the students feel about this ice cream."

Passion is not the only thing that distinguishes the Creamery. At one time, nearly every land-grant college had some type of creamery operation. Many have closed over the years, including fine creameries at West Virginia, Vermont, Virginia Tech, Ohio State, and Purdue. Today, perhaps only a dozen survive. Schools like Wisconsin, North Carolina State, Washington State, and Cornell have outstanding creameries, but all are significantly smaller than Penn State's Creamery, and none have grown the way Penn State's has.

The mystique associated with the Berkey Creamery is not just a matter of passion for ice cream. Its role in the famous Ice Cream Short Course, now directed by Robert Roberts after the 1997 retirement of Arun Kilara, still brings international recognition. The Gram Equipment Co. of Denmark donated a new ice cream freezer to the new Creamery plant. Why would a European company donate a $100,000 piece of equipment to Penn State? Because company officials know that students from all over the world will see and use it in the Ice Cream Short Course. This investment in the future is one more piece of evidence for the remarkable story of the Creamery.

What does the future hold for the Berkey Creamery? Tom Palchak believes the future is bright. With student enrollments steady and applications to attend Penn State rising as never before, with Penn State becoming very much a year-round institution, and with strong support from the Creamery's customers, there is no reason to believe that the future is anything but … well … Peachy.

The Creamery's "Hall of Fame" Flavors

Peachy Paterno

Keeney Beany Chocolate

Made with peaches, nectarine puree, and peach schnapps, Peachy Paterno was created in 1987, after the team's second national championship. The Creamery decided to commemorate Coach Paterno's contributions to higher education and Penn State by naming his favorite peach ice cream for him. The Food Science Club's naming contest drew over 1,000 entries and the Paterno Family looked through them all and made the final selection.

Made with cocoa, bittersweet chocolate chunks, vanilla beans, and vanilla, Keeney Beany Chocolate was created in 1985 to honor ice cream professor par excellence Philip G. Keeney on his retirement as professor emeritus of food science with a new flavor especially beloved of chocoholics. This was highly appropriate because Keeney led research on the chemistry of the cocoa bean and other chocolate-related projects for more than twenty years. At his retirement, the chocolate industry established a $1.5 million endowment at Penn State to study the molecular biology of cocoa.

Cherry Quist

Made with black cherries, cherry sauce, and vanilla, Cherry Quist was created in 1981 to honor John O. Almquist, professor of dairy physiology, who won the Wolf Foundation award in that year for his pioneering work in artificial insemination of livestock. Considered to be the "Nobel Prize of Agriculture," this international honor was recognized by the Creamery by naming Almquist's favorite black cherry ice cream for him. In 1999, the Dairy Breeding Research Center was renamed the Almquist Research Center to honor the man whose work was instrumental in leading the unit to national prominence in the field of reproductive physiology.

WPSU Coffee Break

Made with chocolate, coffee, espresso coffee extract, and vanilla, WPSU Coffee Break was created in 1990 as a special flavor for the twenty-fifth anniversary of then–WPSX-TV, one of America's first public broadcasting systems. In 2005, Penn State Public Broadcasting consolidated call letters into WPSU TV/FM, and the latest Hall of Fame flavor became WPSU Coffee Break. With the growing popularity of coffee and chocolate, this combination of flavors is the perfect treat for news junkies.

47

A Creamery Family Album

Frank Knoll's tenure as Creamery superintendent was the longest on record, from 1905 to 1944. Knoll was originally from Beach Lake, in northeastern Pennsylvania's Wayne County, and enrolled in the creamery course himself in 1903, later working in a Johnstown dairy before returning to Penn State. During those years he distinguished himself as manager and maker of all things dairy, and as a teacher of dairy manufacturing and trusted colleague. Known as a top butter-maker, Frank Knoll oversaw the growth of the Creamery through Patterson Building and into the new Borland Lab.

The photo album the faculty and staff of the Dairy Science Department presented to him on June 12, 1944, remained a treasured keepsake of the family until donated to the University Archives in 2007. Frank Knoll had the good fortune to live another twenty-nine years, serving as a trustee of St. Paul's Methodist Church in State College, and enjoying free time as an avid fisherman. He died in 1973.

Right: Frank Knoll and his bride, J. Frances Budd, taken on their wedding day, May 24, 1900
Facing page: The Knoll children (left to right), Marie, Margaret, and H. Budd, circa 1914

This memento is presented to Frank P. Knoll on the occasion of thirty nine years of faithful service to the State College Creamery and the Pennsylvania State College, by members of the staff and office force of the department of Dairy Husbandry June twelfth, nineteen forty four. With it goes the best wishes and kindest thoughts of each member.

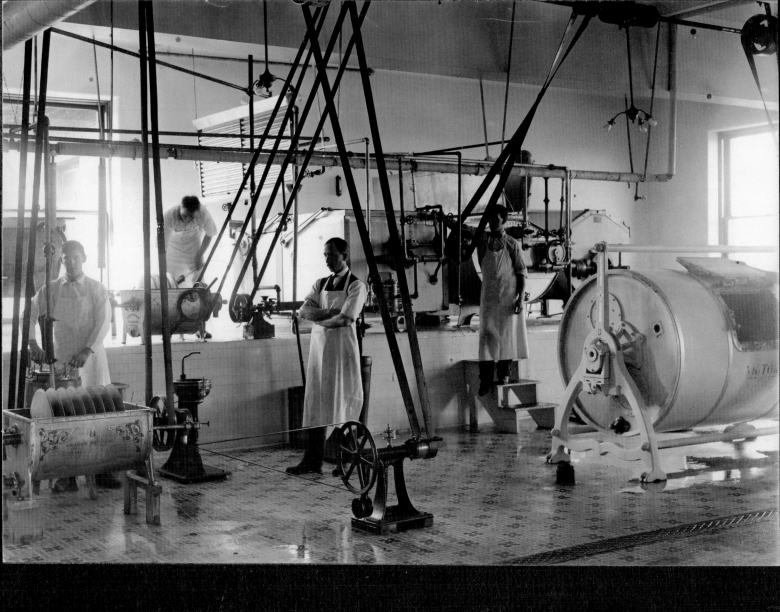

Frank, the instructor.

Facing page: Frank Knoll with butter-making apparatus in Patterson Building ca. 1905
Above: The Borland Lab receiving dock, ca. 1944, with local farm trucks lining up to bring milk and cream into the Creamery for processing

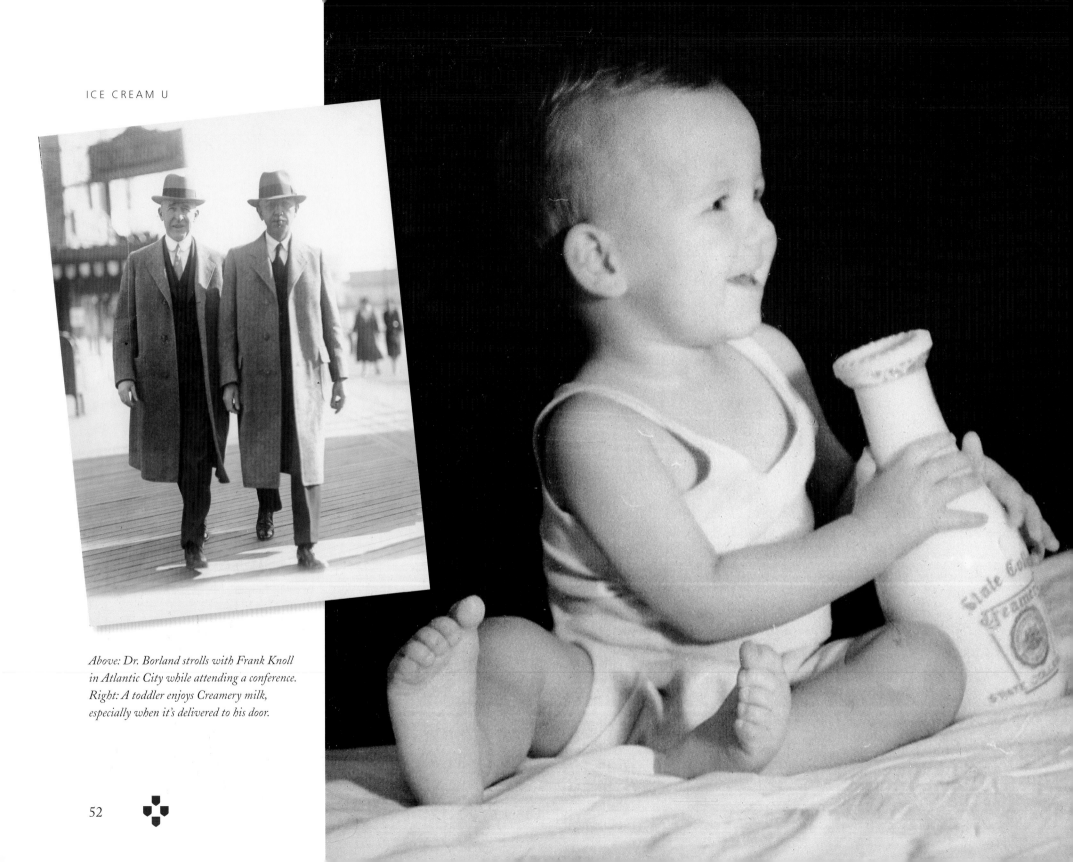

Above: Dr. Borland strolls with Frank Knoll in Atlantic City while attending a conference. Right: A toddler enjoys Creamery milk, especially when it's delivered to his door.

52

Frank Knoll (second from right in bottom row), is joined by faculty and staff of the Dairy Husbandry Department, including Dr. Borland (third from left, bottom row), Carl Dahle (far left, bottom row), Francis J. Doan (second from left, middle row), and Donald Josephson (second from right, top row).

From Pasture to Peachy Paterno:

How Penn State Creamery ice cream is made

1

The Penn State Holstein dairy cows are milked **twice a day, 365 days a year**. At 5:00 a.m. and 5:00 p.m., when their udders are full, the dairy barn workers move 20 cows into the milking parlor at one time. It takes four to five minutes to milk each cow, with as many as **100 cows being milked in one hour** on the vacuum pressure milking units.

2

The milk is transferred by **vacuum pipeline** to a heat exchanger where it is rapidly chilled from nearly 100 degrees to 50 degrees.

3

Milk is moved to the **refrigerated bulk storage tank** where it is kept at approximately 37 degrees until the milk can be collected by a refrigerated tank truck every other day.

4

The 5,000-gallon tank truck collects the refrigerated milk. Before pumping the contents into the **raw milk silo** at the Creamery, a sample is tested for bacteria, antibiotic residue, and milk-fat content.

5

Milk in the silo is removed for various products as needed. A portion of the **raw milk goes through a separator** to produce cream and skim milk.

6

The ingredients for the ice cream mix are combined in the **mixing tanks**: cream, skim milk, powdered milk, sugar and other sweeteners, and small amounts of stabilizers to keep the air-bubble structure together for better texture, and emulsifiers to distribute the fat molecules more evenly for a smooth taste. The fat content of the cream is reduced to 14%, the standard for Penn State's premium ice cream.

7

The mix circulates through the **pasteurizer** to kill harmful bacteria, then is cooled and moved through the **homogenizer** to make the fat globules a uniform, microscopic size.

8

The mix flows into a **24-hour aging tank** cooling to 37 degrees. T allows milk solids to recrystallize and milk f to surround milk proteins.

Day 1

Day 2

5:00 AM   6:00 AM   6:30 AM   1:00 AM   3:00 AM   5:00 AM   5:30 AM   6:00 AM

10

From the flavor vats, ice cream production begins in earnest, as the mix is pumped through the **continuous process freezer**, where **250 gallons of ice cream can be made in an hour**. Air is injected into the mix and liquid cooling pipes rapidly bring the temperature down to 21 degrees.

12

Any **fruit, nuts, or candy** needed for a particular flavor are injected into the frozen ice cream and the completed mix goes through the fillers into 3-gallon tubs, half-gallon "scrounds," pints, and Dixie cups.

14

The ice cream containers are moved to **cold storage rooms**, where they may stay at minus-25 degrees for up to two months.

13

The ice cream containers quickly move to the **Hardening Room**, maintained at minus-35 degrees. There, the ice cream is taken down to 0 degrees over a twelve-hour period. This rapid hardening prevents large water crystals from forming, thus providing a smooth and creamy taste, and also maintains the product's volume in the package.

15

When ice cream is needed, it goes to the **Tempering Freezer** to bring the temperature up to 0 to 5 degrees, which makes it soft enough to be dipped into cones or dishes.

9

The mix enters vats where **liquid flavorings** are added and remains at 37 degrees.

11

The mix flows through a long tube called a **"barrel,"** with blades called **"dashers"** inside, turning constantly to mix the ice cream and scrape away the ice crystals that form on the inside of the barrel. **This is the heart of the process**. The barrel performs the same function as a container in a hand-cranked freezer surrounded by ice and rock salt, with dasher blades constantly turning the mix.

Day 3

Day 4

6:00 AM   6:30 AM   6:40 AM   6:45 AM   7:00 AM   7:00 AM   8:00 AM

The Holstein Dairy Cows of Penn State

Although small numbers of these cows were brought into New York's Hudson Valley by Dutch colonists in the 1620s, today's American herds are descendents of Dutch cows introduced starting in the 1860s. While some historical literature uses the name Holstein-Friesian cattle, those cows bred in America over the last century and a half are now referred to simply as Holsteins; European cows sharing the same origins are known today as Friesians, after the part of the Netherlands where the breed was originally developed. Because so much of the recovered Dutch lowland area was planted in grass, Holsteins were bred to particularly favor the luxuriant grass. The cattle became large-framed, with the average cow being 1,500 pounds.

Holsteins have become the dominant cow in the American dairy production arena primarily because the average Holstein produces more milk than other breeds. Ninety percent of dairy farmers milk at least some Holsteins

Barn to left is one of the new free-stall barns built in 1994, which allows the cows to move freely among bedding, water bowls, and feed troughs, instead of remaining in individual stalls. Two barns above are part of the original 1951-52 installation, now used by dry cows.

and the 22 million registered Holsteins across America represent a significant majority of all U.S. dairy cattle. Average annual production has consistently been over 21,000 pounds of milk per cow. However, this dominance has been a gradual process. In 1920, for example, 11 million Holsteins represented nearly 50 percent of all American dairy cows, with 9.5 million Jerseys, 2 million Guernseys, 0.4 million Ayrshires, and 0.2 million Brown Swiss cows completing the nation's herd.

A century ago, interest in the breed of cow was dictated by production potential. The Guernsey, fawn with white markings, came from the English Channel island of Guernsey to the United States in the 1830s. It was a smaller cow, averaging about 1,100 pounds, and it gave a yellowish milk (later marketed as "Golden Guernsey"), that was almost 50 percent higher in milk fat than the Holstein. The deep yellow cream had very large fat globules and churned easily. The Jersey, from the Channel island of Jersey, came to America in the early 1800s. It was the smallest of cows, averaging about 1,000 pounds, and its milk contained the greatest fat content, 60 percent higher than the Holstein. In the nineteenth century, when almost all milk went into butter and cheese, these were the favorite breeds.

Over the past 75 years, with the rapidly growing dominance of fluid milk sales and changes in production combining milk from different breeds, standardized and homogenized to 3.5 percent fat, the clear advantage of Holsteins in the amount of milk, and thus the actual pounds of fat and protein, they produce has become a market force. The other breeds still have their advocates, of course, and, through various metrics for herd management and return on investment, assert that a case can be made for alternative choices.

Penn State's dairy herd once included purebred representatives of all five of the common breeds of cattle. In 1951–52, new modern dairy barns were built north of Beaver Stadium that contained barns for each of the five breeds. In 1955 the new facilities became operational. However, with changes in the dairy industry, Penn State has followed suit and today, the herd is all Holstein. A century ago, the average production was 5,285 pounds of milk per cow, today it is over 24,000 pounds, showing the dominance of the Holstein as well as improvements to the breed over the years.

Above and left: Milking staff checks to make sure all procedures are complete before releasing cows back to the barns.

Cows in the milking parlor: Twenty cows are milked at one time. Here, the staff member has dipped the teats in an iodine and water solution and is attaching the milking machine. The cow will release up to forty-five pounds of milk in five to six minutes.

Dairy barns and silos are just north of Beaver Stadium.

Read More About It ...

Bezilla, Michael. *Penn State: An Illustrated History*. University Park, Pa.: Penn State University Press, 1985. Available on the Web at: **www.libraries.psu.edu/speccolls/ psua/psgeneralhistory/bezillapshistory/index.htm**

Bezilla, Michael. *The College of Agriculture at Penn State: A Tradition of Excellence*. University Park, Pa.: Penn State University Press, 1987.

Civitello, Linda. *Cuisine and Culture: A History of Food and People*. Second edition. Hoboken, N.J.: John Wiley & Sons, 2008.

DuPuis, E. Melanie. *Nature's Perfect Food: How Milk Became America's Drink*. New York: New York University Press, 2002.

Fletcher, S. W. *Pennsylvania Agriculture and Country Life*. 2 vols. Harrisburg, Pa.: Pennsylvania Historical and Museum Commission, 1950–1955.

Ice Cream Short Course: Proceedings of the Penn State Ice Cream Centennial Conference, May 3–6, 1992. Edited by Manfred Kroger. University Park, Pa.: Department of Food Science, The Pennsylvania State University, 1992.

Kroger, Manfred. *Trends in Food Science: History at Penn State*. Lancaster, Pa.: DES*tech* Publications Inc., 2007.

Schlebeker, John T. *A History of American Dairying*. Chicago: Rand McNally & Co., 1967.

Zurborg, Carl. E. *A History of Dairy Marketing in America*. Columbus, Ohio: National Dairy Shrine, 2005.

Photo credits:
Unless otherwise noted, all photos are property of The Pennsylvania State University.

Greg Grieco, Penn State Department of Public Information: 41, 42 (bottom)

M. Scott Johnson, Penn State Department of University Publications: 37 (right)

Howard Nuernberger, Penn State College of Agricultural Sciences: 13 (bottom), 14

University Archives/Penn State Room, University Libraries: ii (facing title page), vi (facing Acknowl-
edgments), 3 (bottom), 6, 7, 8, 9, 12, 13 (top), 15, 16, 17, 18, 19, 20, 21, 22, 23, 24, 25, 26, 27, 28, 29,
30, 31, 32, 33, 34, 35

Fredric L. Weber, Penn State Department of University Publications: vii (Contents), viii (facing
Introduction), 2, 3 (top), 4, 11, 36, 37 (left), 38, 40, 42 (top left and right), 43, 44, 45, 46, 47, 56, 57,
58/59, 60, 61, 62

Courtesy Knoll family: 48, 49, 50, 51, 52, 53

Courtesy Dee Stout: 39

jupiterimages by Photos.com: 5, 11

Designed by Erin J. Wease, Penn State Department of University Publications
Composed in Adobe Caslon with chapter openings and folios in Frutiger
Printed on 157gsm GoldEast matte text